Maxims extracted from

POOR RICHARD'S ALMANAC

1733-1758

Benjamin Franklin

First published 1732

First published 2018
Copyright © 2018 Aziloth Books

All Rights Reserved. No part of this publication may be reproduced, stored in a retrieval system or transmitted in any form or by any means, electronic, mechanical, photocopying, recording, scanning or otherwise, except under the terms of the Copyright Licensing Agency Ltd, 90 Tottenham Court Road, London, W1P 0LP, UK, without the permission in writing of the Publisher. Requests to the Publisher should be via email to: info@azilothbooks.com.

Every effort has been made to contact all copyright holders. The publisher will be glad to make good in future editions any errors or omissions brought to their attention.

This publication is designed to provide authoritative and accurate information in regard to the subject matter covered. It is sold on the understanding that the Publisher is not engaged in rendering professional services.

British Library Cataloguing in Publication Data

A catalogue record for this book is available from the British Library

ISBN-13: 978-1-911405-59-7

Illustrations:

Front cover: *Benjamin Franklin,* Joseph Duplesis, 1778
Back cover: Front page of *Poor Richard's Almanac*, 1739

Publisher's Note

The reader will find occasional repetitions of the same, or similar, maxims in some of the 26 sections. This was the norm for many such collections of sayings and proverbs in those days.

CONTENTS

INTRODUCTION	4
1733	5
1734	6
1735	9
1736	12
1737	15
1738	19
1739	21
1740	23
1741	25
1742	26
1743	28
1744	30
1745	32
1746	33
1747	34
1748	35
1749	36
1750	37
1751	38
1752	40
1753	41
1754	43
1755	45
1756	47
1757	48
1758	50
Background on *The Way to Wealth*	52
PREFACE TO POOR RICHARD'S 1758 ALMANAC – *The Way to Wealth* (Father Abraham's Speech)	53
BIOGRAPHICAL NOTE	59

INTRODUCTION

Poor Richard's Almanac was a kind of periodical as well as a guide to natural phenomena and the weather. Franklin took his title from *Poor Robin*, a famous English almanac, and from Richard Saunders, a well-known almanac publisher. It was an annual publication that lasted from 1732 to 1758 and achieved huge popularity, with print runs reaching 10,000 per year.

Below, Franklin describes the almanac's origins and the idea behind it.

Aziloth Books

IN 1732 I first publish'd my Almanack, under the name of *Richard Saunders*; it was continu'd by me about twenty-five years, commonly call'd *Poor Richard's Almanac*.[74] I endeavour'd to make it both entertaining and useful, and it accordingly came to be in such demand, that I reap'd considerable profit from it, vending annually near ten thousand. And observing that it was generally read, scarce any neighborhood in the province being without it, I consider'd it as a proper vehicle for conveying instruction among the common people, who bought scarcely any other books; I therefore filled all the little spaces that occurr'd between the remarkable days in the calendar with proverbial sentences, chiefly such as inculcated industry and frugality, as the means of procuring wealth, and thereby securing virtue; it being more difficult for a man in want, to act always honestly, as, to use here one of those proverbs, *it is hard for an empty sack to stand upright*.

These proverbs, which contained the wisdom of many ages and nations, I assembled and form'd into a connected discourse prefix'd to the Almanack of 1757,* as the harangue of a wise old man to the people attending an auction. The bringing all these scatter'd councils thus into a focus enabled them to make greater impression. The piece, being universally approved, was copied in all the newspapers of the Continent; reprinted in Britain on a broadside, to be stuck up in houses; two translations were made of it in French, and great numbers bought by the clergy and gentry, to distribute gratis among their poor parishioners and tenants. In Pennsylvania, as it discouraged useless expense in foreign superfluities, some thought it had its share of influence in producing that growing plenty of money which was observable for several years after its publication.

Benjamin Franklin
Memoirs of Benjamin Franklin, Written by Himself,
Part II, Vol. I, 1793, London.

---

* It was actually 1758. See p. 53, *The Way to Wealth*.

1733

Light purse, heavy heart.

•

He's a Fool that makes his Doctor his Heir.

•

He's gone, and forgot nothing but to say Farewell to his creditors.

•

Hunger never saw bad bread.

•

Great Talkers, little Doers.

•

Fools make feasts and wise men eat 'em.

•

The poor have little, beggars none, the rich too much, enough not one.

•

Eat to live, and not live to eat.*

•

After three days men grow weary, of a wench, a guest, and weather rainy.

•

The proof of gold is fire, the proof of woman, gold; the proof of man, a woman.

•

He that lies down with Dogs, shall rise up with fleas.

•

Distrust & caution are the parents of security.

•

He is ill cloth'd, who is bare of Virtue.

•

Nothing more like a Fool, than a drunken Man.

•

Innocence is its own Defence.

---

* See Molière (1668): "Il faut manger pour vivre, et non pas vivre pour manger." ("*One must eat to live, and not live to eat.*") From Socrates, as quoted by Plutarch: "*Bad men live to eat and drink, and Good men eat and drink to live.*"

1734

You cannot pluck roses without fear of thorns, Nor enjoy fair wife without danger of horns.

•

Without justice, courage is weak.

•

Would you live with ease, Do what you ought, not what you please.

•

Blame-all and Praise-all are two blockheads.

•

Take this remark from Richard poor and lame,
Whate'er's begun in anger ends in shame.

•

What one relishes, nourishes.

•

No man e'er was glorious, who was not laborious.

•

All things are easy to Industry, All things difficult to Sloth.

•

If you ride a Horse, sit close and tight, If you ride a Man, sit easy and light.

•

Don't think to hunt two hares with one dog.*

•

Fools multiply folly.

•

Beauty & Folly are old companions.

•

Better slip with foot than tongue.

•

Hope of gain, lessens pain.

•

Wedlock, as old Men note, hath likened been,
Unto a publick Crowd or common Rout;
Where those that are without would fain get in,
And those that are within would fain get out.
Grief often treads upon the Heels of Pleasure,
Marry'd in Haste, we oft repent at Leisure;
Some by Experience find these Words misplac'd,
Marry'd at Leisure, they repent in Haste.

•

Where there's Marriage without Love, there will be Love without Marriage.

* See Thomas Fuller, *Gnomologia* (1732), #2782.

Be neither silly, nor cunning, but wise.

•

Neither a Fortress nor a Maidenhead will hold out long after they begin to parly.

•

Who pleasure gives, Shall joy receive.

•

All things are cheap to the saving, dear to the wasteful.

•

Would you persuade, speak of Interest, not of Reason.

•

Happy's the Wooing that's not long a doing.

•

Jack Little sow'd little, & little he'll reap.

•

Do good to thy Friend to keep him, to thy enemy to gain him.

•

A good Man is seldom uneasy, an ill one never easy.

•

Teach your child to hold his tongue, he'll learn fast enough to speak.

•

Don't value a man for the Quality he is of, but for the Qualities he possesses.

•

As Charms are nonsense, Nonsense is a Charm.

•

He that cannot obey, cannot command.

•

An innocent Plowman is more worthy than a vicious Prince.

•

He that is rich need not live sparingly,
and he that can live sparingly need not be rich.

•

If you wou'd be reveng'd of your enemy, govern your self.

•

A wicked Hero will turn his back to an innocent coward.

•

Laws like to Cobwebs catch small Flies, Great one break thro' before your eyes.

•

An Egg to day is better than a Hen to-morrow.*

•

Drink Water, Put the Money in your Pocket, and leave the Dry-bellyach in the Punchbowl.

* See Thomas Fuller (physician), *Gnomologia* (1732), #2916.

When 'tis fair be sure to take your Great coat with you.

•

He does not possess Wealth, it possesses him.*

•

Necessity has no Law; I know some Attorneys of the name.

•

Onions can make, ev'n Heirs and Widows weep.

•

Strange, that he who lives by Shifts, can seldom shift himself.

•

As sore places meet most rubs, proud folks meet most affronts.

•

The thrifty maxim of the wary Dutch, is to save all the Money they can touch.

•

He that waits upon Fortune, is never sure of a Dinner.

•

A learned blockhead is a greater blockhead than an ignorant one.

•

Marry your Son when you will, but your Daughter when you can.

•

Avarice and Happiness never saw each other,
how then shou'd they become acquainted.

•

If you woul'd have Guests merry with your cheer,
Be so your self, or so at least appear.

•

Reader, farewel, all Happiness attend thee:
May each New Year better and richer find thee.

---

* See Thomas Fuller (physician), *Gnomologia* (1732), #1125.

1735

Bad Commentators spoil the best of books,
So God sends meat (they say) the devil Cooks.*

•

Approve not of him who commends all you say.

•

By diligence and patience, the mouse bit in two the cable.

•

Full of courtesie, full of craft.

•

Look before, or you'll find yourself behind.

•

A little House well fill'd, a little Field well till'd, and a little Wife well will'd, are great Riches.

•

The poor man must walk to get meat for his stomach,
the rich man to get a stomach to his meat.

•

Eyes and Priests Bear no Jests.

•

The Family of Fools is ancient.

•

Necessity never made a good bargain.

•

If Pride leads the Van, Beggary brings up the Rear.

•

There's many witty men whose brains can't fill their bellies.

•

Weighty Questions ask for deliberate Answers.

•

Be slow in chusing a Friend, slower in changing.

•

Pain wastes the Body, Pleasures the Understanding.

---

* Compare this quote to: "God sends meat, and the Devil sends cooks" by the *Water Poet* John Taylor, *Works*, vol. ii. p. 85 (1630);
"God sendeth and giveth both mouth and the meat", Thomas Tusser, *A Hundred Points of Good Husbandry* (1557); and
"Are these the choice dishes the Doctor has sent us? Is this the great poet whose works so content us? This Goldsmith's fine feast, who has written fine books? Heaven sends us good meat, but the Devil sends cooks?", David Garrick, *Epigram on Goldsmith's Retaliation*. Vol. ii. p. 157.

The cunning man steals a horse, the wise man lets him alone.

•

Keep thy shop, & thy shop will keep thee.

•

The King's cheese is half wasted in parings; but no matter,
'tis made of the peoples milk.*

•

Nothing but Money, Is Sweeter than Honey.

•

Humility makes great men twice honourable.

•

Of learned Fools I have seen ten times ten,
Of unlearned wise men I have seen a hundred.

•

Three may keep a Secret, if two of them are dead.

•

Poverty wants some things, Luxury many things, Avarice all things.

•

A lie stands on 1 leg, the Truth on 2.

•

What's given shines, What's receiv'd is rusty.

•

Sloth and Silence are a Fool's Virtues.

•

There's small Revenge in Words, but Words may be greatly revenged.

•

A man is never so ridiculous by those Qualities that are his own
as by those that he affects to have.

•

Deny Self for Self's sake.

•

Ever since Follies have pleas'd, Fools have been able to divert.

•

It is better to take many Injuries than to give one.

•

Opportunity is the great Bawd.

•

Early to bed and early to rise, makes a man healthy, wealthy and wise.

•

To be humble to Superiors is Duty, to Equals Courtesy, to Inferiors Nobleness.

---

* Compare: "The king's cheese goes half away in parings." James Howell (1659)

Here comes the Orator! with his Flood of Words, and his Drop of Reason.

•

If what most men admire, they would despise,
'Twould look as if mankind were growing wise.

•

The Sun never repents of the good he does,
nor does he ever demand a recompence.

•

An old young man, will be a young old man.

•

Some are weatherwise, some are otherwise.

•

Are you angry that others disappoint you?
Remember you cannot depend upon yourself.

•

One Mend-fault is worth two Find-faults,
but one Find-fault is better than two Make-faults.

1736

He is no clown that drives the plow, but he that doth clownish things.

•

If you know how to spend less than you get, you have the Philosopher's Stone.

•

The good Paymaster is Lord of another man's Purse.

•

Fish & Visitors stink in 3 days.

•

Diligence is the mother of Good-Luck.

•

He that lives upon Hope, dies fasting.

•

Do not do what you would not have known.

•

Never praise your Cyder, Horse, or Bedfellow.

•

Wealth is not his that has it, but his that enjoys it.

•

Tis easy to see, hard to foresee.

•

In a discreet man's mouth, a publick thing is private.

•

Let thy maidservant be faithful, strong, and homely.

•

Keep flax from fire, and youth from gaming.

•

Bargaining has neither friends nor relations.

•

Admiration is the Daughter of Ignorance.

•

There's more old Drunkards than old Doctors.

•

She that paints her face, thinks of her Tail.

•

He that takes a wife, takes care.

•

He that can have Patience, can have what he will.

•

God helps them that help themselves.

Why does the blind man's wife paint herself?

•

None preaches better than the ant, and she says nothing.

•

The absent are never without fault, nor the present without excuse.

•

If wind blows on you thro' a hole, Make your will and take care of your soul.

•

The rotten Apple spoils his Companion.

•

Don't throw stones at your neighbours, if your own windows are glass.

•

The excellency of hogs is fatness, of men virtue.

•

Good wives and good plantations are made by good husbands.

•

Pox take you, is no curse to some people.

•

He that sells upon trust, loses many friends, and always wants money.

•

Gifts burst rocks.

•

Force shites upon Reason's Back.

•

Lovers, Travellers, and Poets, will give money to be heard.

•

He that speaks much, is much mistaken.

•

Creditors have better memories than debtors.

•

Forwarn'd, forearm'd, unless in the case of Cuckolds,
who are often forearm'd before warn'd.

•

Three things are men most liable to be cheated in, a Horse, a Wig, and a Wife.

•

He that lives well, is learned enough.

•

Poverty, Poetry and new Titles of Honour, make Men ridiculous.

•

He that scatters Thorns, let him not go barefoot.

•

There's none deceived but he that trusts.

God heals, and the Doctor takes the Fees.

•

If you desire many things, many things will seem but a few.

•

Mary's mouth costs her nothing, for she never opens it but at others expense.

•

Receive before you write, but write before you pay.

•

I saw few die of Hunger, of Eating 100,000.

•

He that would live in peace & at ease,
Must not speak all he knows, nor judge all he sees.

1737

Note: The following section is difficult for the modern reader to comprehend, due to its use of terms and abbreviations (for monetary units) that have long fallen out of use (especially in the United States). Briefly, the basic unit of currency in Colonial times, in England and in the Colonies, was the pound sterling (designated by the abbreviation *l.*). Twenty Shillings (designated by the abbreviation *s.*) made up a pound; each shilling was worth twelve pennies (designated by the abbreviation *p.*) or pence; thus, there were 240 pence in one pound. A Groat was a silver coin worth four pence. Mickle is a term meaning, "a great amount." "Many a little makes a mickle (Many small amounts accumulate to make a large amount)" was once a familiar proverbial phrase. Finally, pin, as in the phrase "pin money", probably designates a tiny but non-specific amount. The phrase "pin money" referred to an allowance granted by husbands to enable their wives to purchase pins, which were originally a pricey but essential item used by housewives in the making of clothing.

HINTS for those that would be Rich.

The use of Money is all the Advantage there is in having Money.

For 6*l.* a year, you may have Use of 100*l.* a year, if you are a Man of known Prudence and Honesty.

He that spends a Groat a day idly, spends idly above 6*l.* a year, which is the Price of using 100*l.*

He that wastes idly a Groat's worth of his Time per Day, one day with another, wastes the Privilege of using 100*l.* each Day.

He that idly loses 5*s.* worth of time, loses 5*s.* and might as prudently throw 5*s.* in the River.

He that loses 5*s.* not only loses that Sum, but all the Advantage that might be made by turning it in Dealing, which by the time that a young Man becomes old, amounts to a comfortable Bag of Mony.

Again, He that sells upon Credit, asks a Price for what he sells, equivalent to the Principal and Interest of his Money for the Time he is like to be kept out of it: therefore

He that buys upon Credit, pays Interest for what he buys.

And He that pays ready Money, might let that Money out to use: so that
He that possesses any Thing he has bought, pays Interest for the Use of it.

Consider then, when you are tempted to buy any unnecessary Household stuff, or any superfluous thing, whether you will be willing to pay Interest, and Interest upon Interest for it as long as you live; and more if it grows worse by using.

Yet, in buying Goods, 'tis best to pay ready Money, because,

He that sells upon Credit, expects to lose 5 per Cent, by bad Debts; therefore he charges, on all he sells upon Credit, an Advance that shall make up that Deficiency.

Those who pay for what they buy upon Credit, pay their share of this Advance.

He that pays ready Money, escapes or may escape that Charge.

A Penny sav'd is Twopence clear, A pin a day is a Groat a Year. Save & have. Every little makes a mickle.

The greatest monarch on the proudest throne,
is oblig'd to sit upon his own arse.*

•

The Master piece of Man, is to live to the purpose.

•

He that steals the old man's supper, do's him no wrong.

•

A countryman between 2 Lawyers, is like a fish between two cats.

•

He that can take rest is greater than he that can take cities.

•

The miser's cheese is the wholesomest.

•

Love & lordship hate companions.

•

The nearest way to come at glory,
is to do that for conscience which we do for glory.

•

There is much money given to be laught at, though the purchases don't know it;
witness A's fine horse, & B's fine house.

•

He that can compose himself, is wiser than he that composes books.

•

Poor Dick, eats like a well man, and drinks like a sick.

•

After crosses and losses men grow humbler and wiser.

•

Love, Cough, & a Smoke, can't be well hid.

•

Well done is better than well said.

---

* Perhaps a prosaic translation of Michel de Montaigne's earlier aphorism: "Au plus élevé trône du monde, si ne sommes assis que sur notre cul."

He that can travel well afoot, keeps a good horse.

•

There are no ugly Loves, nor handsome Prisons.
No better relation than a prudent & faithful Friend.

•

A Traveller should have a hog's nose, deer's legs, and an ass's back.

•

At the working man's house hunger looks in but dares not enter.

•

A good Lawyer is a bad Neighbour.

•

Certainlie these things agree, the Priest, the Lawyer, & Death all three:
Death takes both the weak and the strong.
The lawyer takes from both right and wrong,
and the priest from the living and the dead has his Fee.

•

The worst wheel of the cart makes the most noise.

•

Don't misinform your Docter nor your Lawyer.

•

I never saw an oft-transplanted tree, nor yet an oft-removed family,
that throve so well as those that settled be.

Three good meals a day is bad living.

•

To whom thy secret thou dost tell, to him thy freedom thou dost sell.*

•

If you'd have a Servant that you like, serve your self.

•

He that pursues two Hares at once, does not catch one and lets t'other go.

•

If you have time don't wait for time.

•

Tell a miser he's rich, and a woman she's old,
you'll get no money of one, nor kindness of t'other.

•

Don't go to the doctor with every distemper, nor to the lawyer with every
quarrel, nor to the pot for every thirst.

---

* Compare to Thomas Fuller (physician), *Gnomologia* (1732), #5184: "To him, that you tell your Secret, you resign your Liberty," and to George Herbert, *Jacula Prudentum* (1651), #508: "He that tells a secret is another's servant," but also see James Howell, *Lexicon Tetraglotton* (1660): "To whom thy secret thou dost tell, to him thy freedom thou dost sell."

The Creditors are a superstitious sect, great observers of set days and times.

•

The noblest question in the world is,
What Good may I do in it?

•

Nothing so popular as GOODNESS.

1738

There are three faithful friends, an old wife, an old dog, and ready money.

Who has deceiv'd thee so oft as thy self?

Read much, but not many books.

Write with the learned, pronounce with the vulgar.

Hast thou virtue? acquire also the graces & beauties of virtue.

Buy what thou hast no need of;
and e'er long thou shalt sell thy necessaries.

If thou hast wit & learning, add to it Wisdom and Modesty.

You may be more happy than Princes, if you will be more virtuous.

If you wou'd not be forgotten
As soon as you are dead and rotten,
Either write things worth reading,
Or do things worth the writing.

Sell not virtue to purchase wealth, nor Liberty to purchase power.

Let thy vices die before thee.*

Keep your eyes wide open before marriage, half shut afterwards.**

The ancients tell us what is best; but we must learn of the moderns what is fittest.

'Tis less discredit to abridge petty charges, than to stoop to petty Gettings.

Since thou art not sure of a minute, throw not away an hour.

Since I cannot govern my own tongue, tho' within my own teeth, how can I hope to govern the tongues of others?

---

* See Thomas Fuller (physician), Introductio ad prudentiam: Part II (1727), #1772.
** See Thomas Fuller (physician), Introductio ad prudentiam: Part II (1727), #1817.

If you do what you should not, you must hear what you would not.

•

Wish not so much to live long as to live well.

•

As we must account for every idle word, so we must for every idle silence.

•

I have never seen the Philosopher's Stone that turns lead into Gold, but I have known the pursuit of it turn a Man's Gold into Lead.

•

Time is an herb that cures all Diseases.

•

Reading makes a full Man, Meditation a profound Man, discourse a clear Man.

•

If any man flatters me, I'll flatter him again; tho' he were my best Friend.

•

Wish a miser long life, and you wish him no good.

•

None but the well-bred man knows how to confess a fault, nor acknowledge himself in an error.

•

Drive thy business; let not that drive thee.

•

There is much difference between imitating a good man, and counterfeiting him.

•

Each year one vicious habit rooted out,
In time might make the worst Man good throughout.

•

Wink at small faults; remember thou hast great ones.

•

Eat to please thyself, but dress to please others.

•

Search others for their virtues, thy self for thy vices.

1739

If thou wouldst live long, live well; for Folly and Wickedness shorten Life.

•

Trust thy self, and another shall not betray thee.

•

He that pays for Work before it's done, has but a pennyworth for twopence.

•

Historians relate, not so much what is done, as what they would have believed.

•

Thou canst not joke an Enemy into a Friend;
but thou may'st a Friend into an Enemy.

•

He that falls in love with himself, will have no Rivals.

•

Let thy Child's first Lesson be Obedience,
and the second may be what thou wilt.

•

Blessed is he that expects nothing, for he shall never be disappointed.

•

Let thy Discontents be Secrets.

•

A Man of Knowledge like a rich Soil, feeds If not a world of Corn,
a world of Weeds.

•

No Resolution of Repenting hereafter, can be sincere.

•

Honour thy Father and Mother,
i.e., Live so as to be an Honour to them tho' they are dead.

•

If thou injurest Conscience, it will have its Revenge on thee.

•

Hear no ill of a Friend, nor speak any of an Enemy.

•

Pay what you owe, and you'll know what's your own.

•

Be not niggardly of what costs thee nothing,
as courtesy, counsel, & countenance.

•

Beware of him that is slow to anger: He is angry for some thing,
and will not be pleased for nothing.

•

Proclaim not all thou knowest, all thou owest, all thou hast, nor all thou canst.
Let our Fathers and Grandfathers be valued for their Goodness,
ourselves for our own.

Industry need not wish.

•

Sin is not hurtful because it is forbidden
but it is forbidden because it's hurtful.

•

Nor is a Duty beneficial because it is commanded,
but it is commanded, because it's beneficial.

•

Great Beauty, great strength, & great Riches, are really & truly of no great Use;
a right Heart exceeds all.

1740

To hear other Peoples Afflictions, every one has Courage enough, and to spare.*

•

An empty bag will not stand upright.

•

Happy that nation, fortunate that age, whose history is not diverting.

•

An open Foe may prove a curse; But a pretended friend is worse.

•

A wolf eats sheep but now and then, Ten Thousands are devour'd by men.

•

Man's tongue is soft, and bone doth lack;
Yet a stroke therewith may break a man's back.

•

The poor have little, Beggars none; the Rich too much, enough not one.

•

Tricks and trechery are the Practice of Fools,
that have not Wit enough to be honest.

•

There are lazy Minds as well as lazy Bodies.

•

Who says Jack is not generous? he is always fond of giving,
and cares not for receiving. What? Why, Advice.

•

Fear not Death; for the sooner we die, the longer shall we be immortal.

•

Those who in quarrels interpose, Must often wipe a bloody nose.

•

Promises may get thee friends,
but Nonperformance will turn them into enemies.

•

In other men we faults can spy,
And blame the mote that dims their eye;
Each little speck and blemish find;
To our own stronger errors blind.

•

Observe all men; thy self most.

---

* Compare this quote to "Nous avons tous assez de force pour supporter les maux d'autrui." ("We all have strength enough to endure the misfortunes of others."), François de la Rochefoucauld, *Reflections: or Sentences and Moral Maxims* (1665-1668), Maxim 19.

Thou hadst better eat salt with the Philosophers of Greece,
than sugar with the Courtiers of Italy.

•

Seek Virtue, and, of that possest, To Providence, resign the rest.

Marry above thy match, and thou'lt get a Master.

•

Fear to do ill, and you need fear naught else.

•

He makes a Foe who makes a jest.

•

Avoid dishonest Gain: No price Can recompence the Pangs of Vice.

•

When befriended, remember it: When you befriend, forget it.

•

Employ thy time well, if thou meanest to gain leisure.

•

A Flatterer never seems absurd: The Flatter'd always take his Word.

•

Lend Money to an Enemy, and thou'lt gain him,
to a Friend and thou'lt lose him.

1741

Learn of the skilful: He that teaches himself, hath a fool for his master.

•

Best is the Tongue that feels the rein:–
He that talks much, must talk in vain;
We from the wordy torrent fly:
Who listens to the chattering Pye?

•

Anger and Folly walk cheek by jole; Repentance treads on both their Heels.

•

Be always asham'd to catch thy self idle.

•

Lying rides upon Debt's back.

•

They who have nothing to be troubled at, will be troubled at nothing.

•

If evils come not, then our fears are vain:
And if they do, Fear but augments the pain.

•

If you would keep your Secret from an enemy, tell it not to a friend.

•

Up, Sluggard, and waste not life; in the grave will be sleeping enough.

•

There are no fools so troublesome as those that have wit.

•

Quarrels never could last long, If on one side only lay the wrong.

•

Let no Pleasure tempt thee, no Profit allure thee, no Ambition corrupt thee,
no Example sway thee, no Persuasion move thee,
to do any thing which thou knowest to be Evil;
So shalt thou always jollily:
for a good Conscience is a continual Christmas Adieu.

1742

Strange! that a Man who has wit enough to write a Satyr;
should have folly enough to publish it.

•

He that hath a Trade, hath an Estate.

•

Have you somewhat to do tomorrow; do it today.

•

Speak and speed: the close mouth catches no flies.

•

Late Children, early Orphans.

•

Ben beats his Pate, and fancys wit will come;
But he may knock, there's no body at home.

•

Ill Customs & bad Advice are seldom forgotten.

•

He that sows thorns, should not go barefoot.

•

When Knaves fall out, honest Men get their goods:

•

When Priests dispute, we come at the Truth.

•

Death takes no bribes.

•

One good Husband is worth two good Wives;
for the scarcer things are the more they're valued.

•

He that riseth late, must trot all day,
and shall scarce overtake his business at night.

•

He that speaks ill of the Mare, will buy her.

•

You will be careful, if you are wise;
How you touch Men's Religion, or Credit, or Eyes.

•

They who have nothing to trouble them, will be troubled at nothing.

•

Against Diseases here, the strongest Fence,
Is the defensive Virtue, Abstinence.

•

If thou dost ill, the joy fades, not the pains;
If well, the pain doth fade, the joy remains.

To err is human, to repent divine, to persist devilish.

•

Industry pays Debts, Despair encreases them.

•

With the old Almanack and the old Year,
Leave thy Vices. tho' never so dear.

•

The Difficulty lies, in finding out an exact Measure; but eat for Necessity, not Pleasure, for Lust knows not where Necessity ends.

•

If thou art dull and heavy after Meat,
it's a sign thou hast exceeded the due Measure;
for Meat and Drink ought to refresh the Body, and make it chearful,
and not to dull and oppress it.

1743

Let all Men know thee, but no man know thee thoroughly:
Men freely ford that see the shallows.

•

How few there are who have courage enough to own their Faults,
or resolution enough to mend them!

•

Men differ daily, about things which are subject to Sense,
is it likely then they should agree about things invisible?

•

Mark with what insolence and pride,
Blown Bufo takes his haughty stride;
As if no toad was toad beside.

•

In prosperous fortunes be modest and wise,
The greatest may fall, and the lowest may rise:
But insolent People that fall in disgrace,
Are wretched and nobody pities their Case.

•

The World is full of fools and faint hearts;
and yet every one has courage enough to bear the misfortunes,
and wisdom enough to manage the Affairs of his neighbor.

•

Beware, beware! he'll cheat 'ithout scruple, who can without fear.

•

Content and Riches seldom meet together,
Riches take thou, contentment I had rather.

•

Speak with contempt of none, from slave to king,
The meanest Bee hath, and will use, a sting.

•

The church, the state, and the poor, are 3 daughters which we should maintain,
but not portion off.

•

A little well-gotten will do us more good,
Than lordships and scepters by Rapine and Blood.

•

Let all Men know thee, but no man know thee thoroughly:
Men freely ford that see the shallows.

•

Tis easy to frame a good bold resolution;
but hard is the Task that concerns execution.

•

Cold & cunning come from the north:
But cunning sans wisdom is nothing worth.

Ah, simple Man! when a boy two precious jewels were given thee,
Time, and good Advice; one thou hast lost, and the other thrown away.

•

The sleeping Fox catches no poultry. Up! up!

•

If you'd be wealthy, think of saving, more than of getting:
The Indies have not made Spain rich, because her Outgoes equal her Incomes.

•

Experience keeps a dear school,
yet Fools will learn in no other.

•

How many observe Christ's Birthday!
How few, his Precepts!
O! 'tis easier to keep Holidays than Commandments.

1744

He that drinks his Cyder alone,
Let him catch his Horse alone.

•

Who is strong?
He that can conquer his bad Habits.

•

Who is rich?
He that rejoices in his Portion.

•

He that has not got a Wife, is not yet a compleat Man.

•

What you would seem to be, be really.

•

If you'd lose a troublesome Visitor, lend him Money.

•

Tart Words make no Friends: a spoonful of honey will catch more flies
than a Gallon of Vinegar.

•

Make haste slowly.

•

Hear Reason, or she'll make you feel her.

•

Give me yesterday's Bread, this Day's Flesh, and last Year's Cyder.

•

God heals, and the Doctor takes the Fees.

•

Sloth (like Rust) consumes faster than Labour wears:
the used Key is always bright.

•

Keep thou from the Opportunity, and God will keep thee from the Sin.

•

Where there's no Law, there's no Bread.

•

As Pride increases, Fortune declines.

•

The same man cannot be both Friend and Flatterer.

•

He who multiplies Riches multiplies Cares.

•

Those who are fear'd, are hated.

The Things which hurt, instruct.

•

A soft Tongue may strike hard.

•

A true Friend is the best Possession.

•

Epitaph on a Scolding Wife by her Husband.
Here my poor Bridget's Corps doth lie, she is at rest,
–and so am I.

1745

Beware of little Expences, a small Leak will sink a great Ship.

•

A light purse is a heavy Curse.

•

Help, Hands; for I have no Lands.

•

It's common for Men to give pretended Reasons instead of one real one.

•

Vanity backbites more than Malice.

•

He's a Fool that cannot conceal his Wisdom.

•

Great spenders are bad lenders.

•

You may talk too much on the best of subjects.

•

No gains without pains.

•

There are no fools so troublesome as those that have wit.

•

Many complain of their Memory, few of their Judgment.*

•

Fools make feasts and wise men eat them.

•

Light heel'd mothers make leaden-heel'd daughters.

•

'Tis easier to prevent bad habits than to break them.

•

Every Man has Assurance enough to boast of his honesty, few of their Understanding.

•

An ounce of wit that is bought,
Is worth a pound that is taught.

•

He that resolves to mend hereafter, resolves not to mend now.

---

* Compare this quote to "Tout le monde se plaint de sa mémoire, et personne ne se plaint de son jugement." ("Everyone blames his memory; no one blames his judgment.") From *Reflections; or Sentences and Moral Maxims* (1665-1678), François de la Rochefoucauld, Maxim 89.

1746

When the Well's dry, we know the Worth of Water.

•

A good Wife and Health, is a Man's best Wealth.

•

A quarrelsome Man has no good Neighbors.

•

Vice knows she's ugly, so puts on her Mask.

•

Women & Wine, Game & Deceit,
Make the Wealth small and the Wants great.

•

It's the easiest Thing in the World for a Man to deceive himself.

•

Virtue and Happiness are Mother and Daughter.

•

Dost thou love Life? then do not squander Time;
for that's the Stuff Life is made of.

•

Good Sense is a Thing all need, few have, and none think they want.

•

Want of Care does us more Damage than Want of Knowledge.

•

The Sting of a Reproach, is the Truth of it.

•

The most exquisite Folly is made of Wisdom spun too fine.

1747

There's a time to wink as well as to see.

•

There is no Man so bad, but he secretly respects the Good.

•

Courage would fight, but Discretion won't let him.

•

We are not so sensible of the greatest Health as of the least Sickness.

•

A good Example is the best sermon.

•

A Father's a Treasure; a Brother's a Comfort; a Friend is both.

•

He that won't be counsell'd, can't be help'd.

•

Write Injuries in Dust,
Benefits in Marble.

•

What maintains one Vice would bring up two Children.

•

Better is a little with content than much with contention.

•

A slip of the foot you may soon recover;
But a slip of the Tongue you may never get over.

•

What signifies your Patience, if you can't find it when you want it.

•

Time enough, always proves little enough.

•

It is wise not to seek a Secret, and Honest not to reveal it.

•

A Mob's a Monster;
Heads enough, but no Brains.

•

The Devil sweetens Poison with Honey.

•

He that cannot bear with other People's Passions, cannot govern his own.

1748

Lost Time is never found again.
•
Life with Fools consists in Drinking;
With the wise Man, Living's Thinking.
•
Liberality is not giving much but giving wisely.
•
The second Vice is Lying; the first is Running in Debt.
•
When you're good to others, you are best to yourself.
•
Half Wits talk much but say little.
•
If Jack's in love, he's no judge of Jill's Beauty.
•
Most Fools think they are only ignorant.
•
Pardoning the Bad, is injuring the Good.
•
He is not well-bred, that cannot bear Ill-Breeding in others.

1749

Wise Men learn by other's harms; Fools by their own.

•

The end of Passion is the beginning of Repentance.

•

Words may shew a man's Wit, but Actions his Meaning.

•

'Tis a well spent penny that saves a groat.

•

Many Foxes grow grey, but few grow good.

•

Content makes poor men rich;
Discontent makes rich men poor.

•

Drink does not drown Care, but waters it, and makes it grow faster.

•

If your head is wax, don't walk in the sun.

•

Having been poor is no shame, but being ashamed of it, is.

•

The wise Man draws more Advantage from his Enemies,
than the Fool from his Friends.

•

All would live long, but none would be old.

•

Declaiming against Pride, is not always a Sign of Humility.

•

Doing an Injury puts you below your Enemy;
Revenging one makes you but even with him;
Forgiving it sets you above him.

•

Most of the Learning in use, is of no great Use.

•

A Man in a Passion rides a mad Horse.

•

Reader farewel, all Happiness attend thee;
May each New-Year, better and richer find thee.

1750

There are three things extreamly hard,
Steel, a Diamond and to know one's self.

•

Hunger is the best Pickle.

•

He is Governor that governs his Passions,
and he a Servant that serves them.

•

Wouldst thou confound thine Enemy, be good thy self.

•

Pride is as loud a Beggar as Want, and a great deal more saucy.

•

Pay what you owe, and what you're worth you'll know.

•

Many a Man thinks he is buying Pleasure,
when he is really selling himself a Slave to it.

•

He that can bear a Reproof, and mend by it,
if he is not wise, is in a fair way of being so.

•

Clean your Finger, before you point at my Spots.

•

He that spills the Rum, loses that only;
He that drinks it, often loses both that and himself.

•

Genius without education is like silver in the mine.

•

Little Strokes Fell great Oaks.

•

Many would live by their Wits, but break for want of Stock.

•

Hide not your Talents, they for Use were made.

•

What's a Sun-Dial in the Shade!

•

What signifies knowing the Names, if you know not the Natures of Things.

•

Glass, China, and Reputation, are easily crack'd,
and never well mended.

1751

Pray don't burn my House to roast your Eggs.

•

Many a Man would have been worse,
if his Estate had been better.

•

We may give Advice, but we cannot give Conduct.

•

He that is concious of a Stink in his Breeches,
is jealous of every Wrinkle in another's nose.

•

Most People return small Favors, acknowledge middling ones,
and repay great ones with Ingratitude.

•

'Tis easier to suppress the first Desire, than to satisfy all that follow it.

•

If your Riches are yours,
why don't you take them with you to t'other World?

•

What more valuable than Gold?
Diamonds.
Than Diamonds? Virtue.

•

If worldly Goods cannot save me from Death,
they ought not to hinder me of eternal Life.

•

Today is Yesterday's Pupil.

•

'Tis great Confidence in a Friend to tell him your Faults,
greater to tell him his.

•

Ambition often spends foolishly what Avarice had wickedly collected.

•

Great Estates may venture more;
Little Boats must keep near Shore.

•

Nice Eaters seldom meet with a good Dinner.

•

Not to oversee Workmen, is to leave them your Purse open.

•

The Wise and Brave dares own that he was wrong.

•

Cunning proceeds from Want of Capacity.

The Proud hate Pride – in others.

•

Who judges best of a Man, his Enemies or himself?

•

Drunkenness, that worst of Evils,
makes some men Fools, some Beasts, some Devils.

•

'Tis not a Holiday that's not kept holy.

1752

Kings have long Arms, but Misfortune longer:
Let none think themselves out of her Reach.

•

For want of a Nail the Shoe is lost; for want of a Shoe, the Horse is lost; for want of a Horse the Rider is lost.

•

The busy Man has few idle Visitors;
to the boiling Pot the Flies come not.

•

'Tis more noble to forgive, and more manly to despise,
than to revenge an Injury.

•

A Brother may not be a Friend, but a Friend will always be a Brother.

•

Meanness is the Parent of Insolence.

•

A Temper to bear much, will have much to bear.

•

Great Merit is coy, as well as great Pride.

•

An undutiful Daughter, will prove an unmanageable Wife.

•

Old Boys have their Playthings as well as young Ones;
the Difference is only in the Price.

•

The too obliging Temper is evermore disobliging itself.

•

Hold your Council before Dinner;
the full Belly hates Thinking as well as Acting.

•

The Brave and the Wise can both pity and excuse;
when Cowards and Fools shew no Mercy.

•

Ceremony is not Civility; nor Civility Ceremony.

•

If Man could have Half his Wishes, he would double his Troubles.

•

Children and Princes will quarrel for Trifles.

•

Success has ruin'd many a Man.

1753

'Tis against some Mens Principle to pay Interest,
and seems against others Interest to pay the Principal.

•

Setting too good an Example is a Kind of Slander seldom forgiven;
'tis Scandalum Magnatum.

•

A great Talker may be no Fool, but he is one that relies on him.

•

It is not Leisure that is not used.

•

Paintings and Fightings are best seen at a distance.

•

If you would reap Praise you must sow the Seeds,
Gentle Words and useful Deeds.

•

Ignorance leads Men into a Party,
and Shame keeps them from getting out again.

•

Many have quarrel'd about Religion, that never practis'd it.

•

Sudden Power is apt to be insolent, Sudden Liberty saucy;
that behaves best which has grown gradually.

•

He that best understands the World, least likes it.

•

Haste makes Waste.

•

Anger is never without a Reason, but seldom with a good One.

•

He that is of Opinion Money will do every Thing,
may well be suspected of doing every Thing for Money.*

•

An ill Wound, but not an ill Name, may be healed.

•

When out of Favour, none know thee; when in, thou dost not know thyself.

•

God, Parents, and Instructors, can never be requited.

---

* Compare this quote to "They who are of opinion that Money will do every thing, may very well be suspected to do every thing for Money.", George Savile, *Moral Thoughts and Reflections* (1750).

If you have no Honey in your Pot,
have some in your Mouth.

•

Serving God is Doing Good to Man,
but Praying is thought an easier Service,
and therefore more generally chosen.

•

Nothing humbler than Ambition, when it is about to climb.

•

Gifts much expected, are paid, not given.

1754

The first Degree of Folly, is to conceit one's self wise;
the second to profess it; the third to despise Counsel.

•

Take heed of the Vinegar of sweet Wine, and the Anger of Good-nature.

•

Cut the Wings of your Hens and Hopes,
lest they lead you a weary Dance after them.

•

The Cat in Gloves catches no Mice.

•

In Rivers and bad Governments,
the lightest Things swim at top.

•

If you'd know the Value of Money, go and borrow some.

•

The horse thinks one thing, and he that saddles him another.

•

Love thy Neighbor; yet don't pull down your Hedge.

•

In the Affairs of this World Men are saved,
not by Faith, but by the Want of it.

•

Friendship cannot live with Ceremony, nor without Civility.

•

The learned Fool writes his Nonsense in better Language
than the unlearned; but still 'tis Nonsense.

•

A Child thinks 20 Shillings and 20 Years can scarce ever be spent.

•

You may give a Man an Office, but you cannot give him Discretion.

•

He that doth what he should not, shall feel what he would not.

•

Little Rogues easily become great Ones.

•

You may sometimes be much in the wrong,
in owning your being in the right.

•

Friends are the true Sceptres of Princes.

•

Where Sense is wanting, every thing is wanting.
For Age and Want save while you may,

No Morning Sun lasts a whole Day.

•

Many Princes sin with David, but few repent with him.

•

He that hath no ill Fortune will be troubled with good.

1755

A Man without a Wife,
is but half a Man.

•

Speak little, do much.

•

When the Wine enters, out goes the Truth.

•

If you would be loved, love and be lovable.

•

The honest Man takes Pains, and then enjoys Pleasures;
the Knave takes Pleasure, and then suffers Pains.

•

Think of three Things, whence you came, where you are
going, and to whom you must account.

•

There was never a good Knife made of bad Steel.

•

The Wolf sheds his Coat once a Year, his Disposition never.

•

Who is wise? He that learns from every One.

•

Who is powerful? He that governs his Passions.

•

Who is rich? He that is content.
Who is that?
Nobody.

•

The Day is short, the Work great, the Workmen lazy,
the Wages high, the Master urgeth;
Up, then, and be doing.

•

The Doors of Wisdom are never shut.

•

Much Virtue in Herbs, little in Men.

•

When you taste Honey, remember Gall.

•

Being ignorant is not so much a Shame,
as being unwilling to learn.

•

God gives all Things to Industry.

Diligence overcomes Difficulties,
Sloth makes them.

•

Neglect mending a small Fault, and 'twill soon be a great one.

•

A long Life may not be good enough, but a good Life is long enough.

•

Be at War with your Vices, at Peace with your Neighbours,
and let every New Year find you a better Man.

1756

Love your Enemies, for they tell you your Faults.

•

Vain-Glory flowereth, but beareth no Fruit.

•

Laws too gentle are seldom obeyed; too severe, seldom executed.

•

Love, and be loved.

•

A wise Man will desire no more, than what he may get justly,
use soberly, distribute cheerfully, and leave contentedly.

•

A false Friend and a Shadow, attend only while the sun shines.

•

To-morrow, every fault is to be amended;
but that To-morrow never comes.

•

Plough deep, while Sluggards sleep;
And you shall have Corn, to sell and to keep.

•

He that sows Thorns, should never go barefoot.

•

Laziness travels so slowly, that Poverty soon overtakes him.

•

Sampson with his strong Body, had a weak Head,
or he would not have laid it in a Harlot's Lap.

•

To be proud of Knowledge, is to be blind with Light;
to be proud of Virtue, is to poison yourself with the Antidote.

•

Get what you can, and what you get, hold;
'Tis the Stone that will turn all your Lead into Gold.

•

An honest Man will receive neither Money nor Praise, that is not his Due.

•

Saying and Doing, have quarrel'd and parted.

•

Tell me my Faults, and mend your own.

1757

God helps them that help themselves.

•

Dost thou love life?
Then do not squander time, for that is the stuff life is made of.

•

Early to bed and early to rise, Makes a man healthy, wealthy, and wise.

•

Plough deep while sluggards sleep.

•

Never leave that till to-morrow which you can do to-day.

•

Three removes are as bad as a fire.

•

Little strokes fell great oaks.

•

A little neglect may breed mischief: for want of a nail the shoe was lost; for want of a shoe the horse was lost; and for want of a horse the rider was lost.

•

He that goes a borrowing goes a sorrowing.

•

A man may, if he knows not how to save as he gets,
keep his nose to the grindstone.

•

Vessels large may venture more, But little boats should keep near shore.

•

It is hard for an empty bag to stand upright.

•

Experience keeps a dear school, but fools will learn in no other.

•

Many a Man's own Tongue gives Evidence against his Understanding.*

•

Anger warms the Invention, but overheats the Oven.

•

It is Ill-Manners to silence a Fool, and Cruelty to let him go on.**

---

* Compare this quote to "Most men make little other use of their Speech than to give evidence against their own Understanding.", George Savile, *Moral Thoughts and Reflections* (1750).

** Compare this quote to "It is Ill-manners to silence a Fool, and Cruelty to let him go on.", George Savile, *Moral Thoughts and Reflections* (1750).

Men take more pains to mask than mend.*

•

One To-day is worth two To-morrows.

•

The way to be safe is never to be secure.**

•

Dally not with other Folks' Women or Money.

•

Work as if you were to live 100 years,
Pray as if you were to die To-morrow.

•

Pride breakfasted with Plenty, dined with Poverty, supped with Infamy.

•

Act uprightly, and despise Calumny;
Dirt may stick to a Mud Wall, but not to polish'd Marble.

•

The Tongue offends, and the Ears get the Cuffing.

---

* Compare this quote to "Men take more pains to hide than to mend themselves." George Savile, *Miscellaneous Thoughts and Reflections* (1750).

**Aphorism quoted by Francis Quarles.

1758

When you're an Anvil, hold you still;
When you're a Hammer, strike your Fill.

•

When Knaves betray each other, one can scarce be blamed, or the other pitied.

•

Fools need Advice most, but wise Men only are the better for it.

•

Silence is not always a Sign of Wisdom, but Babbling is ever a Mark of Folly.

•

Great Modesty often hides great Merit.

•

You may delay, but Time will not.

•

Virtue may not always make a Face handsome,
but Vice will certainly make it ugly.

•

Content is the Philosopher's Stone, that turns all it touches into Gold.

•

Statement on the value of contentment.

•

He that's content, hath enough;
He that complains, has too much.

•

Half the Truth is often a great Lie.*

•

The first Mistake in publick Business, is the going into it.

•

The Way to see by Faith, is to shut the Eye of Reason:
The Morning Daylight appears plainer when you put out your Candle.**

•

Good-Will, like the Wind, floweth where it listeth.

•

In a corrupt Age, the putting the World in order would breed Confusion;
then e'en mind your own Business.

---

* Compare this quote to "Half the Truth is often as arrant a Lye, as can be made.", George Savile, *Miscellaneous Thoughts and Reflections* (1750).

** The first portion of this sentence is often quoted without the context provided by the complete statement.

To serve the Publick faithfully, and at the same time please it entirely,
is impracticable.
•
Rob not God, nor the Poor, lest thou ruin thyself;
the Eagle snatcht a Coal from the Altar, but it fired her Nest.
•
With bounteous Cheer,
Conclude the Year.

Background on *The Way To Wealth*

For the last publication of *Poor Richard's Almanac* in 1758, Benjamin Franklin wished to reiterate to his readers the inciteful advice that Poor Richard had dispensed over the years. Franklin did this by engaging the services of another character, Father Abraham, whose statement, *The Way to Wealth,* encapsulated many of the aphorisms cited by Poor Richard in his 26 almanacs – a sort of "collected wisdom."*

In a public place, at "an auction of public goods," Richard Saunders hears this wise old man quote his advice to the listening crowd. Poor Richard realises, with humility, that these maxims did not come from any inherent wisdom on his part, but were merely his observations – "the gleanings that I had made of the sense of all ages and nations." He resolves immediately "to be the better for the echo of it" and encourages his readers to do the same.

---

* In 1760, it was issued separately under the title *Father Abraham's Speech.*

PREFACE TO POOR RICHARD'S ALMANAC, 1758

THE WAY TO WEALTH
Father Abraham's Speech

COURTEOUS READER,

I have heard that nothing gives an author so great pleasure, as to find his works respectfully quoted by others. Judge, then, how much I must have been gratified by an incident I am going to relate to you. I stopped my horse, lately, where a great number of people were collected at an auction of merchants' goods. The hour of the sale not being come, they were conversing on the badness of the times; and one of the company called to a plain, clean, old man, with white locks, 'Pray, Father Abraham, what think you of the times? Will not those heavy taxes quite ruin the country! How shall we be ever able to pay them? What would you advise us to?'

Father Abraham stood up, and replied, "If you would have my advice, I will give it you in short; 'for a word to the wise is enough,' as Poor Richard says." They joined in desiring him to speak his mind, and, gathering round him, he proceeded as follows:

'Friends,' says he, 'the taxes are indeed very heavy; and, if those laid on by the government were the only ones we had to pay, we might more easily discharge them; but we have many others, and much more grievous to some of us. We are taxed twice as much by our idleness, three times as much by our pride, and four times as much by our folly; and from these taxes the commissioners cannot ease or deliver us by allowing an abatement. However, let us hearken to good advice, and something may be done for us; "God helps them that help themselves," as Poor Richard says.

I. 'It would be thought a hard government that should tax its people one-tenth part of their time to be employed in its service: but idleness taxes many of us much more; sloth, by bringing on diseases, absolutely shortens life.

"Sloth, like rust, consumes faster than labour wears, while the used key is always bright," as Poor Richard says. "But, dost thou love life? then do not squander time, for that is the stuff life is made of," as Poor Richard says. How much more than is necessary do we spend in sleep! forgetting that, "the sleeping fox catches no poultry, and that there will be sleeping enough in the grave," as Poor Richard says.

"If time be of all things the most precious, wasting time must be" as Poor Richard says, "the greatest prodigality;" since, as he elsewhere tells us, "Lost time is never found again; and what we call time enough, always proves little enough." Let us then up and be doing, and doing to the purpose: so by diligence shall we do more with less perplexity. "Sloth makes all things difficult, but industry all easy; and he that riseth late, must trot all day, and shall scarce overtake his business at night; while laziness travels so slowly, that poverty soon overtakes him. Drive thy business, let not that drive thee; and early to bed, and early to rise, makes a man healthy, wealthy, and wise," as Poor Richard says.

'So what signifies wishing and hoping for better times? We may make these times better, if we bestir ourselves. "Industry need not wish, and he that lives upon hope will die fasting. There are no gains without pains; then help hands, for I have no lands;" or if I have, they are smartly taxed. "He that hath a trade, hath an estate; and he that hath a calling, hath an office of profit and honour," as Poor Richard says; but then the trade must be worked at, and the calling well followed, or neither the estate nor the office will enable us to pay our taxes.

If we are industrious, we shall never starve; for "at the working man's house hunger looks in, but dares not enter." Nor will the bailiff or the constable enter, for "industry pays debts, while despair increaseth them." What, though you have found no treasure, nor has any rich relation left you a legacy. "Diligence is the mother of good luck, and God gives all things to industry. Then plow deep, while sluggards sleep, and you shall have corn to sell and to keep." Work while it is called to-day, for you know not how much you may be hindered to-morrow. "One today is worth two to-morrows," as Poor Richard says, and farther, "Never leave that till to-morrow, which you can do to-day."

If you were a servant, would you not be ashamed that a good master should catch you idle? Are you then your own master? be ashamed to catch yourself idle, when there is so much to be done for yourself, your family, your country, and your king. Handle your tools without mittens: remember, that "The cat in gloves catches no mice," as Poor Richard says. It is true, there is much to be done, and, perhaps, you are weak-handed: but stick to it steadily, and you will see great effects; for "Constant dropping wears away stones; and by diligence and patience the mouse ate in two the cable; and little strokes fell great oaks."

'Methinks I hear some of you say, "Must a man afford himself no leisure?" I will tell thee, my friend, what Poor Richard says, "Employ thy time well, if thou meanest to gain leisure; and, since thou art not sure of a minute, throw not away an hour." Leisure is time for doing something useful; this leisure the diligent man will obtain, but the lazy man never; for "A life of leisure and a life of laziness are two things. Many, without labour, would live by their wits only, but they break for want of stock;" whereas industry gives comfort, and plenty, and respect. "Fly pleasures and they will follow you. The diligent spinner has a large shift; and now I have a sheep and a cow, every body bids me good-morrow."

II. 'But with our industry we must likewise be steady, settled, and careful, and oversee our own affairs with our own eyes, and not trust too much to others: for, as Poor Richard says,

"I never saw an oft-removed tree,
Nor yet an oft-removed family,
That throve so well as those that settled be."

And again, "Three removes are as bad as a fire," and again, "Keep thy shop, and thy shop will keep thee:" and again, "If you would have your business done, go; if not, send." And again:

*"He that by the plow would thrive,
Himself must either hold or drive."*

'And again, "The eye of the master will do more work than both his hands:" and again, "Want of care does us more damage than want of knowledge;" and again: "Not to oversee workmen, is to leave them your purse open."

'Trusting too much to others' care is the ruin of many; for, "In the affairs of this world, men are saved, not by faith, but by the want of it:" but a man's own care is profitable; for, "If you would have a faithful servant, and one that you like, serve yourself. A little neglect may breed great mischief; for want of a nail the shoe was lost; for want of a shoe the horse was lost; and for want of a horse the rider was lost;" being overtaken and slain by the enemy; all for want of a little care about a horse-shoe nail.*

III. 'So much for industry, my friends, and attention to one's own business; but to these we must add frugality, if we would make our industry more certainly successful. A man may if he knows not how to save as he gets, "keep his nose all his life to the grindstone, and die not worth a groat at last. A fat kitchen makes a lean will;" and,

*"Many estates are spent in the getting,
Since women for tea forsook spinning and knitting,
And men for punch forsook hewing and splitting."*

"If you would be wealthy, think of saving, as well as of getting. The Indies have not made Spain rich, because her out-goes are greater than her incomes."

'Away, then, with your expensive follies, and you will not then have so much cause to complain of hard times, heavy taxes, and chargeable families; for,

*"Women and wine, game and deceit,
Make the wealth small, and the want great."*

And farther, "What maintains one vice, would bring up two children." You may think perhaps, that a little tea, or a little punch now and then, diet a little more costly, clothes a little finer, and a little entertainment now and then, can be no great matter; but remember, "Many a little makes a mickle." Beware of little expences; "A small leak will sink a great ship," as Poor Richard says; and again, "Who dainties love shall beggars prove;" and moreover, "Fools make feasts, and wise men eat them." Here you are all got together to this sale of fineries and nick-nacks. You call them goods; but, if you do not take care, they will prove evils to some of you. You expect they will be sold cheap, and, perhaps, they may for less than they cost; but, if you have no occasion for them, they must

---

* Earlier proverb, compare "For want of a nail the shoe is lost, for want of a shoe the horse is lost, for want of a horse the rider is lost." George Herbert, *Jacula Prudentum* (1651) No. 499.

be dear to you. Remember what poor Richard says, "Buy what thou hast no need of, and ere long thou shalt sell thy necessaries." And again, "At a great pennyworth pause a while," he means, that perhaps the cheapness is apparent only, and not real; or the bargain, by straitening thee in thy business, may do thee more harm than good. For, in another place, he says, "Many have been ruined by buying good pennyworths." Again, "It is foolish to lay out money in a purchase of repentance;" and yet this folly is practised every day at auctions, for want of minding the Almanack. Many a one, for the sake of finery on the back, have gone with a hungry belly, and half starved their families; "Silks and satins, scarlet and velvets, put out the kitchen fire," as Poor Richard says. These are not the necessaries of life; they can scarcely be called the conveniences: and yet only because they look pretty, how many want to have them? By these, and other extravagancies, the genteel are reduced to poverty, and forced to borrow of those whom they formerly despised, but who, through industry and frugality, have maintained their standing; in which case it appears plainly, that "A ploughman on his legs is higher than a gentleman on his knees," as Poor Richard says. Perhaps they have had a small estate left them, which they knew not the getting of; they think "it is day, and will never be night:" that a little to be spent out of so much is not worth minding; but "Always taking out of the meal-tub, and never putting in, soon comes to the bottom," as Poor Richard says; and then, "When the well is dry, they know the worth of water." But this they might have known before, if they had taken his advice. "If you would know the value of money, go and try to borrow some; for he that goes a borrowing, goes a sorrowing," as Poor Richard says; and, indeed, so does he that lends to such people, when he goes to get it in again. Poor Dick farther advises, and says,

"Fond pride of dress is sure a very curse,
Ere fancy you consult, consult your purse."

'And again, "Pride is as loud a beggar as Want, and a great deal more saucy." When you have bought one fine thing, you must buy ten more, that your appearance may be all of a piece; but Poor Dick says, "It is easier to suppress the first desire, than to satisfy all that follow it." And it is as truly folly for the poor to ape the rich, as for the frog to swell, in order to equal the ox.

"Vessels large may venture more,
But little boats should keep near shore."

It is, however, a folly soon punished: for, as Poor Richard says, "Pride that dines on vanity, sups on contempt; Pride breakfasted with Plenty, dined with Poverty and supped with Infamy." And, after all, of what use is this pride of appearance, for which so much is risked, so much is suffered? It cannot promote health, nor ease pain; it makes no increase of merit in the person, it creates envy, it hastens misfortune.

'But what madness it must be to run in debt for these superfluities? We are offered, by the terms of this sale, six months credit; and that, perhaps, has induced some of us to attend it, because we cannot spare the ready money, and hope now to be fine without it. But, ah! think what you do when you run in debt; you give to another power over your liberty. If you cannot pay at the time, you will be ashamed to see your creditor; you will be in fear when you speak to him; you will make poor pitiful sneaking excuses, and, by degrees, come to lose your veracity, and sink into base, downright lying; for, "The second vice is lying, the first is running in debt," as Poor Richard says; and again, to the same purpose, "Lying rides upon Debt's back:" whereas a free-born Englishman ought not to be ashamed nor afraid to see or speak to any man living. But poverty often deprives a man of all spirit and virtue. "It is hard for an empty bag to stand upright."

What would you think of that prince, or of that government, who should issue an edict forbidding you to dress like a gentleman or gentlewoman, on pain of imprisonment or servitude? Would you not say that you were free, have a right to dress as you please, and that such an edict would be a breach of your privileges, and such a government tyrannical? And yet you are about to put yourself under that tyranny, when you run in debt for such dress! Your creditor has authority, at his pleasure, to deprive you of your liberty, by confining you in gaol for life, or by selling you for a servant, if you should not be able to pay him. When you have got your bargain, you may, perhaps, think little of payment; but, as Poor Richard says, "Creditors have better memories than debtors; creditors are a superstitious sect, great observers of set days and times." The day comes round before you are aware, and the demand is made before you are prepared to satisfy it; or, if you bear your debt in mind, the term, which at first seemed so long, will, as it lessens, appear extremely short: "Time will seem to have added wings to his heels as well as his shoulders. Those have a short Lent, who owe money to be paid at Easter." At present, perhaps, you may think yourselves in thriving circumstances, and that you can bear a little extravagance without injury; but

"For age and want save while you may,
No morning sun lasts a whole day."

'Gain may be temporary and uncertain; but ever, while you live, expense is constant and certain; and "It is easier to build two chimneys, than to keep one in fuel," as Poor Richard says: so, "Rather go to bed supper-less, than rise in debt,"

Get what you can, and what you get hold,
'Tis the stone that will turn all your lead into gold.

And when you have got the Philosopher's stone, sure you will no longer complain of bad times, or the difficulty of paying taxes.

IV. 'This doctrine, my friends, is reason and wisdom; but, after all, do not depend too much upon your own industry, and frugality, and prudence, though excellent things; for they may all be blasted without the blessing of Heaven; and therefore, ask that blessing humbly, and be not uncharitable to those that at present seem to want it, but comfort and help them. Remember, Job suffered, and was afterwards prosperous.

'And now to conclude, "Experience keeps a dear school, but fools will learn in no other," as Poor Richard says, and scarce in that; for it is true, "We may give advice, but we cannot give conduct." However, remember this, "They that will not be counselled cannot be helped;" and farther, that "If you will not hear Reason, she will surely rap your knuckles," as Poor Richard says.'

Thus the old gentleman ended his harangue. The people heard it, and approved the doctrine, and immediately practised the contrary, just as if it had been a common sermon; for the auction opened, and they began to buy extravagantly.

I found the good man had thoroughly studied my Almanacks, and digested all I had dropt on those topics during the course of twenty-five years. The frequent mention he made of me must have tired any one else; but my vanity was wonderfully delighted with it, though I was conscious that not a tenth part of the wisdom was my own, which he ascribed to me; but rather the gleanings that I had made of the sense of all ages and nations. However, I resolved to be the better for the echo of it; and, though I had at first determined to buy stuff for a new coat, I went away, resolved to wear my old one a little longer. Reader, if thou wilt do the same, thy profit will be as great as mine.

I am, as ever, thine to serve thee,

Richard Saunders

BIOGRAPHICAL NOTE
Benjamin Franklin (1706-1790)

American statesman, philosopher, and writer, was one of a numerous family. His father was a soap-boiler at Boston, where Franklin was born. He was apprenticed at the age of 13 to his brother, a printer, who treated him harshly. After various changes, during which he lived in New York, London, and Philadelphia, he at last succeeded in founding a successful business as a printer. He also started a newspaper, *The Gazette*, which was highly popular, *Poor Richard's Almanac*, and the *Busybody Papers*, in imitation of the *Spectator*. After holding various minor appointments, he was made deputy Postmaster-General for the American Colonies. In 1757 he went to London on some public business in which he was so successful that various colonies appointed him their English agent. In the midst of his varied avocations he found time for scientific investigation, especially with regard to electricity. For these experiments, he became known over the civilised world, and was loaded with honours. In 1762 he returned to America, and took a prominent part in the controversies which led to the Revolutionary War and the independence of the Colonies. In 1776 he was U.S. Minister to France, and in 1782 was a signatory of the treaty which confirmed the independence of the States. He returned home in 1785, and, after holding various political offices, retired in 1788, and died in 1790. His autobiography is his chief contribution to literature, and is of the highest interest.

John W. Cousin
A Short Biographical Dictionary of English Literature (1910)

AZILOTH BOOKS

Aziloth Books publishes a wide range of titles ranging from hard-to-find esoteric books – *Parchment Books* – to classic works on fiction, politics and philosophy – *Cathedral Classics*. Our newest venture is *Aziloth Books Children's Classics*, with vibrant new covers and illustrations to complement some of the world's very best children's tales. All our imprints are offered to the reader at a competitive price and through as many mediums and outlets as possible.

We are committed to excellent book production and strive, whenever possible, to add value to our titles with original images, maps and author introductions. With the premium on space in most modern dwellings, we also endeavour – within the limits of good book design – to make our products as slender as possible, allowing more books to be fitted into a given bookshelf area.

We are a small, approachable company and would love to hear any of your comments and suggestions on our plans, products, or indeed on absolutely anything.

Aziloth Books, Rimey Law, Rookhope, Co. Durham, DL13 2BL, England.
t: 01388-517600 e: info@azilothbooks.com w: www.azilothbooks.com

Cathedral Classics hosts an array of classic literature, from erudite ancient tomes to avant-garde, twentieth-century masterpieces, all of which deserve a place in your home. All the world's great novelists are here, Jane Austen, Dickens, Conrad, Arthur Machen and Henry James, brushing shoulders with such disparate luminaries as Sun Tzu, Marcus Aurelius, Kipling, Friedrich Nietzsche, Machiavelli, and Omar Khayam. A small selection is detailed below:

Herland	Charlotte Perkins Gilman
With Her in Ourland	Charlotte Perkins Gilman
Frankenstein	Mary Shelley
The Time Machine; The Invisible Man	H. G. Wells
Three Men in a Boat	Jerome K Jerome
The Rubaiyat of Omar Khayyam	Omar Khayyam
A Study in Scarlet	Arthur Conan Doyle
The Sign of the Four	Arthur Conan Doyle
The Picture of Dorian Gray	Oscar Wilde
Flatland	Edwin A. Abbott
The Coming Race	Bulwer Lytton
The Great God Pan	Arthur Machen
Beyond Good and Evil	Friedrich Nietzsche
England, My England	D. H. Lawrence
The Castle of Otranto	Horace Walpole
Self-Reliance, & Other Essays (series1&2)	Ralph W. Emmerson
The Art of War	Sun Tzu
A Shepherd's Life	W. H. Hudson
The Double	Fyodor Dostoyevsky
To the Lighthouse; Mrs. Dalloway	Virginia Woolf
The Sorrows of Young Werther	Johann W. Goethe
Demian: the story of a youth	Herman Hesse
Analects	Confucius
Beowulf	Anonymous
Plain Tales From The Hills	Rudyard Kipling
The Subjection of Women	John Stuart Mill
Silas Marner	George Eliot
Rights of Man	Thomas Paine
Progress and Poverty	Henry George
Captain Blood	Rafael Sabatini
Captains Courageous	Rudyard Kipling
The Meditations of Marcus Aurelius	Marcus Aurelius
The Social Contract	Jean Jacques Rousseau
War is a Racket	Smedley D. Butler
The Dead	James Joyce
The Old Wives' Tale	Arnold Bennett

Obtainable at all good online and local bookstores.
View Aziloth Books' full list at: www.azilothbooks.com

Parchment Books AZILOTH

Parchment Books enshrines the concept of the oneness of all true religious traditions – that "the light shines from many different lanterns". Our list below offers titles from both eastern and western spiritual traditions, including Christian, Judaic, Islamic, Daoist, Hindu and Buddhist mystical texts, as well as books on alchemy, hermeticism, paganism, etc..

By bringing together such spiritual texts, we hope to make esoteric and occult knowledge more readily available to those ready to receive it. We do not publish grimoires or any titles pertaining to the left hand path. Titles include:

The Prophet	Khalil Gibran
The Madman: His Parables and Poems	Khalil Gibran
Abandonment to Divine Providence	Jean-Pierre de Caussade
Corpus Hermeticum	G. R. S. Mead (trans.)
The Holy Rule of St Benedict	St. Benedict of Nursia
The Confession of St Patrick	St. Patrick
The Outline of Sanity	G. K. Chesterton
An Outline of Occult Science	Rudolf Steiner
The Dialogue Of St Catherine Of Siena	St. Catherine of Siena
Esoteric Christianity	Annie Besant
Thought-Forms*	Annie Besant
The Teachings of Zoroaster	Shapurji A. Kapadia
The Spiritual Exercises of St. Ignatius	St. Ignatius of Loyola
Daemonologie	King James of England
A Dweller on Two Planets	Phylos the Thibetan
The Imitation of Christ	Thomas à Kempis
The Interior Castle	St. Teresa of Avila
Songs of Innocence & Experience*	William Blake
The Marriage of Heaven & Hell*	William Blake
The Secret of the Rosary	St. Louis Marie de Montfort
From Ritual to Romance	Jessie L. Weston
The God of the Witches	Margaret Murray
Kundalini – an occult experience	George S. Arundale
The Kingdom of God is Within You	Leo Tolstoy
The Trial and Death of Socrates	Plato
A Textbook of Theosophy	Charles W. Leadbetter
Chuang Tzu: Daoist Teachings	Chuang Tzu
Practical Mysticism	Evelyn Underhill
Tao Te Ching (Lao Tzu's Book of the Way)	Tzu, Lao
The Most Holy Trinosophia	Le Comte de St.-Germain
Tertium Organum	P. D. Ouspensky
Totem and Taboo	Sigmund Freud
The Kebra Negast	E. A. Wallis Budge
Esoteric Buddhism	Alfred Percy Sinnett

* With colour illustrations

Obtainable at all good online and local bookstores.
View Aziloth Books' full list at: www.azilothbooks.com

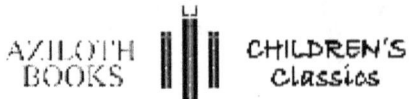

Aziloth Books is passionate about bringing the very best in children's classics fiction to the next generation of book-lovers. We believe in the transforming power of children's books to encourage a life-long love of reading, and publish only the best authors and illustrators. With its original design and outstanding quality, our highly successful list has something to suit every age and interest. Titles include:

The Railway Children	Edith Nesbit
Anne of Green Gables	Lucy Maud Montgomery
What Katy Did	Susan Coolidge
Puck of Pook's Hill	Rudyard Kipling
The Jungle Books	Rudyard Kipling
Just So Stories	Rudyard Kipling
Alice Through the Looking Glass	Charles Dodgson
Alice's Adventures in Wonderland*	Charles Dodgson
Black Beauty	Anna Sewell
The War of the Worlds	H. G Wells
The Time Machine	H. G .Wells
The Sleeper Awakes	H. G. Wells
The Invisible Man	H. G. Wells
The Lost World	Sir Arthur Conan Doyle
Gulliver's Travels*	Jonathan Swift
Catriona (David Balfour)	Robert Louis Stevenson
The Water Babies	Charles Kingsley
The First Men in the Moon	Jules Verne
The Secret Garden	Frances Hodgson Burnett
A Little Princess	Frances Hodgson Burnett
Peter Pan*	J. M. Barrie
The Song of Hiawatha*	Henry W. Longfellow
Tales from Shakespeare	Charles and Mary Lamb
The Story of My Life (with photo album)	Helen Keller
The Wonderful Wizard of Oz	L. Frank Baum

*Illustrations in colour

Obtainable at all good online and local bookstores.
View Aziloth Books' full list at: www.azilothbooks.com

www.ingramcontent.com/pod-product-compliance
Lightning Source LLC
Chambersburg PA
CBHW061249040426
42444CB00010B/2317